CHIPPY CHIPMUNK

Parties in the Garden

*Written and photographed
by Kathy M. Miller*

In memory of my parents for all our shared laughter.

To Jeff for a lifetime of love and support.

I would like to thank Arian Hungaski, Mardi and Rebecca Metzger, Laurie Goodrich, Wendy Cunningham, Donna Sweigert, Jessica Dzurek, Dana Harlos, Cynthia Mensch and Tirah Keal for their help with text editing.

Copyright © 2009 Kathy M. Miller

Published by:

Celtic Sunrise
PO Box 174
New Ringgold, PA 17960
570 943 2102

www.celticsunrise.com

www.chippychipmunk.com

First Edition   10 9 8 7 6 5 4 3 2

Miller, Kathy M.

Chippy Chipmunk Parties in the Garden

Chipmunk / Nature / Humor
For children 4 & older and the young at heart

Summary: A story based on delightful photographs of a Chipmunk's charming antics while he explores a garden.

Photographed, Written & Designed in Schuylkill County, Pennsylvania
Book Layout by Rob Mull Advertising & Design
Prepress production in Ohio
Printed in China

ISBN-13 978-0-9840893-0-7
ISBN-10 0-9840893-0-6
Library of Congress Control Number: 2009905378

Chippy Chipmunk awoke from his long winter nap. Feeling hungry, he scampered up to the top of a big rock and listened for signs of danger.

Bluebirds
and cardinals
sang their sweet
songs of spring.

Munch, munch, munch

went the cottontail rabbit.

Chippy set off to explore the garden.

He hopped
on a chair
and bounded
up a bush.

He ran up and down
a tree where he met...

...a bushy gray squirrel
who was cleaning
his tail.

He danced cheerfully
around the flowers
that tickled his nose.

He stretched up high
on the tips of his toes.

"Yippee!" Chippy chirped, discovering a soft patch of leaves. He stuffed his mouth full and dashed off to his secret burrow.

"These will make a nice comfy bed."

He covered his burrow
with stones he collected from
an underground drainage pit.

How do you
suppose he
carried up
those stones?

Cheek pouches can carry just about anything!

Foraging for food,
Chippy zigzagged
through plants.

He always stayed
alert for signs
of predators.

He surprised a flicker who was feeding on ants.

"Ants! Yuck!" squealed Chippy.
"Grubs are *my* favorite bugs."

Peeking through the garden blossoms he sniffed around for a scrumptious nut, seed or berry.

He even stayed out when it rained.

Every so often he felt

ITCHY.

Using his hind foot he scratched himself vigorously just like a dog or cat.

Peek-a-boo!

Suddenly he felt a vibration.

"Uh-oh," thought Chippy. "I would make a tasty meal for a snake."

He sat **very** still.

It was only a box turtle
wandering slowly through the grass.

She let out a big yawn

and continued on her way.

Chippy felt thirsty, so he
darted over to the birdbath.
He stretched his body over the
edge and slurped up the cool water.

Determined to find food, he scooted to the top of a branch to get a better look. Then he spotted something great.

"Hooray!" he shouted. "It's party time!"

A chickadee,

a downy woodpecker,

a nuthatch,

a titmouse,

and a blue jay

were having a peanut party!

Chippy quickly stopped hunting for acorns because he *just couldn't wait* to go to the peanut party.

He wagged his tail

side to *side*

as he hatched

his plan.

His feet gripped the pole and up he flew. With a flying leap he landed on the feeder, crawled inside and retrieved his prize.

With a hop, skip and a jump he went speeding back to one of his secret hiding places.

He stashed
his bounty in
his burrow.

Back and forth
he ran to the feeder
until his burrow
and tummy were
full.

Now it's
time to take
a chipmunk
bath!

He licked his paws to clean his face and
whisked his tail through his mouth.

He didn't forget to
wash behind his ears.

Then he stretched
out his legs and gave
each a good scrub.

Chippy was heading back
across the garden when
all of a sudden he saw
the most terrifying sight!

A red-tailed
hawk was diving
straight towards
him!

Run, Chippy! Run!

"You didn't really think he would catch me, did you?"

"Let's Party!"

Chipmunk cheek pouches can hold 6 acorns or over 30 sunflower seeds!

They can collect over 100 acorns per hour and can store a year's worth of food.

Solitary critters, they live alone most of their lives.

Sometimes they sing just for fun!

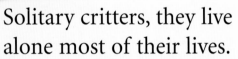

They can build elaborate burrows with multiple tunnels, chambers and entrances.

They know to store only non-perishable food.

They conceal the 2 inch burrow entrances by plugging them with dirt.

Chipmunk predators include: cats, hawks, snakes and foxes.

Reference: Eastern Chipmunks: Secrets of Their Solitary Lives by Lawrence Wishner